Mary —

Good luck in all you do.

Sincerely,
Jim H.

Skies and Chasms

POEMS

James Richard Hansen

authorHOUSE

AuthorHouse™
1663 Liberty Drive
Bloomington, IN 47403
www.authorhouse.com
Phone: 833-262-8899

© 2022 James Richard Hansen. All rights reserved.

No part of this book may be reproduced, stored in a retrieval system, or transmitted by any means without the written permission of the author.

Published by AuthorHouse 08/09/2022

ISBN: 978-1-6655-6803-6 (sc)
ISBN: 978-1-6655-6804-3 (e)

Library of Congress Control Number: 2022915129

Print information available on the last page.

Any people depicted in stock imagery provided by Getty Images are models, and such images are being used for illustrative purposes only.
Certain stock imagery © Getty Images.

This book is printed on acid-free paper.

Because of the dynamic nature of the Internet, any web addresses or links contained in this book may have changed since publication and may no longer be valid. The views expressed in this work are solely those of the author and do not necessarily reflect the views of the publisher, and the publisher hereby disclaims any responsibility for them.

Contents

An Afternoon 1
Communion 2
Wonder 3
Morning Bouquet 4
Perspective 5
Everyday Heroes 6
Antidote 7
Pathetique by Tchaikovsky 8
Spotlight 9
An Orange and Scarlet Cloud 10
Singing 11
Freedom 12
Another World 13
Staying Grounded? 14
Corinne 15
Struggling 16
Imagination and Reality 17
Life 18
Victoria 19
The Nutcracker 20
The Silence 21
Rapt Attention 22
Ruthe 23
The Beach 24
The Eye 25
Panacea 26
On a Starry Night 27

An Avalanche of Sky 28
Demons 29
The Road 30
Fighting 31
Great Americans 32
Cycle of Salvation (Survival?) 33
Writing 34
Clarity 35

Love Poems for Kristen

Under the Moonlight 39
The Good Life 40
Miracles 41
Strange Lands 42
Connected Rings 43
Kristen's Eyes 44
The Haven 45
Journey 46
Liquid Love 47
Finding Inspiration 48
In Your Garden of Love 49
Floating 50
A Reason for Living 51
Glimpse 52

For my wife Kristen. After 17 years, she still has
not proven to me that she is not an angel.

For the many people who are important to me,
including some who have left us:
My niece Corinne, Narendra, Ruthe, and Victoria.

An Afternoon

Sun
Ocean
Clear sky
Gleaming sunlight
on the dark-turquoise Pacific,
electric diamonds glittering
and blinding me with ecstasy.
I'm bathing in the riches of the universe.

Communion

The great mountains cast their glory
over the valley in strangely shaped shadows.
The trees and meadows shine like jewels
in the irregular light.
I hear the songs of several birds
and see deer and squirrels.
Wildflowers and a shallow, limpid stream
add to the grandeur.

Hiking in this masterpiece,
I commune not only with nature,
but with the universe–
and with myself.

Wonder

Stars gaze at me
while I wonder at the wonder
of the universe.
Galaxies speak to me in light,
and darkness informs my peace.
Nothing can prevent me
from loving space and all of nature,
especially humanity.
Even with all its foibles and failures,
the beauty of all existence
is transcendent.
The nature of nature
propels me to rapture,
and I fly among the stars
beholding the infinitude of beauty.

Morning Bouquet

The dawn light shines through my glass door
and lights my room with a celestial glow.
I sit at my computer writing,
but take a break to gaze
at the flowers in our glorious garden.
Roses, carnations, and daffodils
create a striking bouquet
with which to start my day.
Anytime the morning sun creates this glow
in my office and our garden outside,
I am seeing a bit of paradise.

Perspective

Sunset turns the cirrus clouds
crimson and peach.
Wind reshapes them into myriad forms:
some geometric,
some bizarre,
some wildly windblown.
As I absorb the view, I am grateful
for the gifts that make it possible:
nature,
love of nature,
sight,
life.

I must remember
to focus on the good.

Everyday Heroes

For Nalini and Narendra

Nalini's thin figure
belies her inner strength.
Having lost her husband Narendra,
she journeys through life mostly broken.
But she continues to charm the world.
Her family, friends, and work
give her many opportunities
to fill the hearts of others,
as they fill hers.

The entire world depends
on everyday heroes
like Nalini and Narendra–
their endless labor,
their dependability,
their devotion to those they serve.
They seldom get the rewards
they truly deserve.
Without them,
the world would halt.

Antidote

As I stroll down the beach,
the breeze brushes my hair
and caresses my face.
The tide brings easy waves
that flow onto the beach
and spread across the sloping sand.
The wet sand comforts my bare feet.
I absorb the beauty of the setting sun
and the spectacular panorama.
Here I find inner peace,
an antidote to a turbulent world.

Pathetique by Tchaikovsky

Moody and intense,
surging from the deepest ocean
to the stratosphere and back,
it captured me the first time I heard it.
It was Tchaikovsky's favorite, as well.
When I haven't heard it in a while,
I start to crave its unparalleled
drama, darkness, pathos, and joy.
He creates incomprehensible beauty
and gut-wrenching sadness,
all within a few minutes.

What would the world be
without art like his?

Spotlight

I feel the gaze
of the moon on my face.
It focuses mostly on my eyes.
The moonlight,
though typically not so intense,
nearly blinds me with its energy.
In the darkness of the surrounding sky,
the moon is like a spotlight
on me and my life.
I feel I don't measure up.
There seem to be so many ways
I don't measure up.

Will I ever?

An Orange and Scarlet Cloud

I step onto the beach
and feel the warmth of the summer sun
and the light, salty breeze
caressing my face and stirring my hair.
I walk to the shore,
wade into shallow water,
and sink into soft sand.
The Pacific is true to its name—
barely a ripple disturbs
the scintillating surface in the distance.
Light waves lap the shore
as the resplendent sun
gleams off the glassy sea.

A few hours pass.
The orange and scarlet sunset dominates.
I focus on the stunning parade
of colors and windswept clouds
that complement the spectacular sun.
After half an hour of devouring the vision,
it ends, and I walk to my car,
floating on an orange and scarlet cloud.

Singing

I revel in the blessing of morning,
a new day crowned and showcased
by a resplendent, deep-orange sun
surrounded by a sky of deep azure
and white, puffy clouds.
Fresh, crisp air exhilarates and inspires.
The grass I stand on sparkles
with iridescent dew,
while abundant flowers and trees
glow in the morning sun.

The deep orange begins to fade,
and the sun begins to assume
its usual orange-white brilliance.
The song of my day,
begun with a magnificent sunrise,
becomes reality,
and I begin to sing.

Freedom

In my intense drive for freedom,
I stagger and sway and stumble
over obstacles and recoil in fear
of my enemies.
I throw myself toward my goal,
knowing I must succeed
or die.

I will never live without freedom.

Another World

As I settle into sleep,
I feel the rush of dreams
beckoning.
I leave this world
in a flood of visions
and stimulating sounds,
piquant aromas
and the tantalizing touch
of another world.

But my perceptions
quickly turn to horrors.
I want to flee, but can't.
I don't escape till morning,
when I wake in a sweat,
trembling and terrified,
trying to grab hold
of the familiar world.

Staying Grounded?

The star danced around the moon,
flew through its icy halo,
and landed on a cloud.
Other clouds spread their wings
and danced across the sky with the star.
When I asked to join them,
the star replied,
"Don't you want to stay grounded?"
I said, "No, I want to fly."
The clouds grabbed my hands
and pulled me up,
and we danced all night.

Corinne

A life of physical
and emotional pain–
with little relief–
cut short.
She wrote poetry,
but died before publishing.
Like other poets,
she was highly sensitive,
and paid the price.
Her sweet nature
made her vulnerable
to life's vicissitudes.
She couldn't endure.

Struggling

Underwater in the sea of life,
I struggle.
Strong undercurrents
pulled me under,
and I was unable to prevent
my plunge.
But searching inside myself,
I found a reservoir
of strength and willpower
that allowed me to move
closer to salvation.
I can see the surface now.
I can see sunlight
and the promise of life.

Imagination and Reality

The sun disappears
to circle the globe,
and stars slowly shift
from invisibility in daylight
to brilliance in darkness.
Dozens of stars
and hints of the Milky Way
pull me toward an adventure in space.
I leave the comfort of our patio
for a journey among the galaxies.

When I return,
our home is the same–
warm, welcoming, and wonderful.
My imagination enriches my life,
but my reality is better.

Life

The sounds and sights of the Pacific,
the brush of the wind,
the chill of the rain,
the wet sand under my feet.
As I stroll the beach,
the weather beats me down
and lifts me up.
I float in ecstasy,
but the downward pull
of the storm creates inner darkness.
The best of life; life's pain.
I try to reconcile the opposites,
and, knowing I can't,
continue with life.

Victoria

Why did you have to go?
You suffered so,
but we wanted you to win.
Did you win in the end?

I think of you every day–
the way you spoke
with authority and wisdom,
the way you cared,
the way you supported me and others
through some very rough times.

Goodbye, Victoria.
Know that we love you,
that we tried, and try,
to care as much as you did.

The Nutcracker

While I am in the stratosphere
listening to Tchaikovsky,
my flight dips a bit
when I think of the real world.
I return to flight, then the real world,
up and down like my moods.
But Tchaikovsky wins,
and I soar into the wonderland
that is as fresh and moving
as it must have been when he created it
over a century ago.

The Silence

came to me
like a blasting train.
I put my fingers in my ears
so I could hear my thoughts,
but all I heard was silence.
My mind is never silent.

The road back to sanity was fraught
with potholes and ruts
and sharp curves and deadly hazards.
But as my journey evolved,
the silence grew softer,
and my mind began to speak again.

I listened intently.

Rapt Attention

As sunlight dazzles my eyes,
my blindness is surpassed
only by my rapture.
The sunset ignites my imagination.
I see many worlds of stunning beauty,
all more gorgeous
than the one I am actually looking at.

As my passion subsides
and my senses return,
other parts of the real sunset
capture my attention:
orange, pink, and crimson clouds
stretched across the skyscape
in countless shapes and sizes;
the placid Pacific in rich turquoise;
sunrays visible in the light clouds
that look like a scene from a movie
depicting God looking down from heaven.

The only thing missing
is the rest of the universe,
which I refuse to notice.

Ruthe

A miracle on two feet,
she won tennis championships
with her husband as a senior
and lived another 30 years.
But the real miracle lived inside her.
Her unmistakable dignity
commanded respect.
And with character to spare
and warmth to match it,
she charmed people everywhere.

Goodbye, great friend.

The Beach

The sound and sense of the ocean
lapping at my feet,
the chill of the water,
sand twisting and turning and sifting
between my toes,
cool, salty wind brushing my face
and stirring my hair.
I sink into the experience.
Cirrus clouds glow yellow and rose
and stretch across the sunset.
The sun descends the celestial staircase
through an incandescent portal of clouds
on its way to the other side of the world.

Darkness replaces dusk,
stars and moon replace sun,
and fatigue replaces energy
as my evening catharsis ends.

The Eye

A constant eye is on me.
I feel its presence and its vision
as if it were touching me.
I want to escape, run, fly away.
But the eye won't let me.
It will watch me
and pull me back with its tentacles.
Then it will take away more of my freedoms.

Panacea

The sun drops, like my feelings.
Not knowing why, I look to the sky
to find the source of my distress.
But all I see is beauty.

Is this my multilayered answer?

On a Starry Night

moonlight flows onto mountains
in shadowy silver
and reflects off a crystal lake
with an otherworldly glow.
Stars frame the moon
like tiny diamonds on an ebony bed.
A few gossamer clouds stretch
across the luminous sky
in a dramatic light show.
Silhouettes of pines are barely visible
and look like dark, triangular ghosts.

My mind is inundated
by the eerie beauty.
I want more.

An Avalanche of Sky

The sun sets in an avalanche of orange and crimson.
I devour the panorama and feel the sun
as though it were acting directly on my emotions.
When it has dropped below the horizon,
I sink into sand on my back and gaze
at the intensifying moon and stars.
A cool breeze begins to pick up,
and I begin to cool down,
and drift off.

Demons

As I drift into dreamland,
the demons start coming–
demons from the previous day,
demons from early life,
demons from my imagination,
demons from nowhere.
I cope as well as I can
with the dark side,
but only waking saves me.

The Road

As I wander down the road of life,
my solitude is surpassed
only by my desire to flee.
I want to escape to the light
on wings of friendship.
But the light could be treacherous,
and my wings are those of Icarus.
I don't want to fall
into the dark sea of oblivion.
My dilemma never ends.

Fighting

Spellbound by the moon,
I soon became possessed
and had to fight to stay sane.
The pain didn't leave me,
but neither did my mind.
I fought through life
knowing that every fight
could be my last.
But that's in the past.

Now, I often bask in sunlight,
feeling its warmth
and seeing the bright light
in my mind's eye.

The glass is three-quarters full.

Great Americans

For Drs. Cordie and Tania W.

Battle-scarred—but not from war—
he overcame it all with help from Jesus.
With irrepressible enthusiasm,
he works to heal the world.

Behind every great man is a great woman.
She doubles as doctor and mother,
and, with a huge heart,
warms everyone around her.

Together, they carry their message
to everyone who will listen.

Cycle of Salvation (Survival?)

Rain seems to seep through my skin
and cool my blood.
I stand in the storm as a porous being
and feel the rain soothe my soul.
But when the troubles of my day
return to mind,
I am overcome by a tempest of emotion.
I feel the burn
of the acid of anger and pain.

I try to cope.
I try to let go of the acid
and find comfort
in the healing moisture from above.
I try to rediscover inner peace,
as the storm outside of me continues.

Writing

As I drifted down with the sun,
the crimson sky matched the blood
coming from my spirit. I had survived,
but I was wounded to my core.

As the sun sank below the horizon,
my spirit slowly rose with the moon–
as it often does–
and once again I could face
my responsibility:
my life is written by my mind and my heart.

Clarity

As I rise through the clouds into space,
the clouds of my day recede.
I feel one with the darkness.
Only when I am free of the day
do my unity and totality become clear.
To fly through space as a free spirit
and see the stars and galaxies
is enough to make life worth living.
But many, many things
make life worth living.
And as I return to Earth,
these other things become clear, as well.

Love Poems
for Kristen

Under the Moonlight

you looked at me
and I was spellbound.
Your eyes resembled the moon itself,
mesmerizing and bright.
I thought I was losing my freedom,
but I was finding myself.

Now we are under moonlight again,
but this time as husband and wife,
wishing upon all the stars in the universe
that we will be together forever.

The Good Life

For Valentine's Day

Under the mask of daily life,
my love for you grows
every time you smile.
I feel my eyes glow
when I hear your mellifluous voice.
My body quivers when we embrace.
Like someone entering the pearly gates,
I eagerly await your words of love.
At these moments,
life is superb.

Miracles

When I think of my love for you,
the sun flares with brilliance.
Stars turn night to day.
Nature's beauty doubles.

But when you say you love me,
my joy surpasses these miracles.

When we met, the universe grew
to make room for our love.

As time progresses, we progress,
and our bond becomes indestructible.

Strange Lands

The sun drops for the day,
and tiny drops of silvery light
begin to fill the sky.
On this moonless night,
light for my journey
comes from the stars.
My imagination flies to a place
I have never seen before.
I know I will return because
I always have.
And because my stellar wife
awaits my return from the stars.

Connected Rings

For our wedding anniversary

The moon uses our rings
to connect our souls.
Instead of losing ourselves
in becoming one,
we are two in one,
unique but inseparably joined.
We revolve around our love–
a heavenly sphere
filled with magical songs
of adoration and commitment,
sung in the voices of our lives.

Kristen's Eyes

For Kristen on her birthday

Her sapphires sparkle brilliantly,
incandescent light
illuminating my eyes with love.
I feel their passion
even when I can't see them.

Malicious thoughts are foreign to her.
She finds it easy to be good.
Her compassion shows
in her beautiful sapphires–
and her life.

The Haven

For Valentine's Day

When you came into my life,
I felt like I was flying–
soaring into your heart,
and you into mine.
We created a haven–
an open, warm, welcoming
sanctuary of salvation
from the suffering of the world.
We will be here forever,
wanting nothing but to remain
in each other's arms,
searching for ways to express
the unimaginable intensity
of our love.

Journey

As she gracefully descends the staircase,
I feel the softness of her steps,
the waves of her blond hair,
the wisps of her diaphanous gown.
When she reaches the bottom
and embraces me,
I feel the power of her love.
I soar into another world where
no one is wanting,
no one is in pain,
no one is anything but the true self.
I take her with me on this journey,
to which she is already accustomed.

Liquid Love

For Kristen on her birthday

A waterfall floods our hearts
with bracing, pristine spring water
that carries love from nature's reserve.
The source deep in the backcountry
is God's wellspring of happiness.
From the deep basin containing the liquid love,
God's angels keep the goodness flowing.
You were born of that spring,
the endless reservoir
that continues to give the world
untainted goodness
through the presence of your spirit.

Finding Inspiration

Inspiration falls with the rain.
I soak up as much as I can,
but the inspiration dissipates
as the rain evaporates.

So I often need more.
Fortunately, I have you, my love.

In Your Garden of Love

I walk around your arrangement
of roses, lilacs, and irises,
appreciating the spectacle
from every possible angle.
I want to dive into the flowers
and swim in their beauty and fragrance.
But I don't need to.
I have you.
I have your wonderful reality
in a form that never fades,
that never lies dormant in winter.
And you return my love
and make my life wonderful.

Floating

For Valentine's Day

Floating above the Earth,
I feel the warmth of the sun,
the refreshing moisture of the clouds,
the soothing wind.
I feel free.
I want to float in the heavens
forever.
But I know you are waiting on Earth,
so I return home
and float in the heaven of your love.

A Reason for Living

For our wedding anniversary

Rose petals pale next to your spirit.
Sunset on the beach is magical,
but normal compared with you.
I am blinded by your resplendence;
it could make a blind man see.
I have never known a reason for living
so clear, so compelling, so complete
as our love.
As we continue to create our destiny,
I will continue to grow and thrive
in the glow of our love.
You will simply shine
like the angel you have always been.

Glimpse

For Kristen on her birthday

When we are silent,
I hear a rhapsody of love
played by the echo of your heartbeat,
the purr of your mellifluous voice,
the whispering wings of your angelic spirit.

When we close our eyes,
I see your glowing smile,
your radiant blond hair,
your lips softly saying,
"I love you."

When we open our eyes,
and when we listen once more,
I realize that all I'd seen and heard
was but a glimpse
of the reality that is you.

About the Author

James Richard Hansen was born in Denver, Colorado, and moved to California at age twenty. He earned a B.A. in mathematics from California State University, Fresno, and an A.A.S. in accounting/data processing from Heald College. He has worked as a tutor and an IRS tax examiner, among other jobs. He has been writing poetry for over thirty years and has published four previous collections: Progression (2001); JAD (2004); Within and Without (2017); and Words To Breathe By (2020). He lives in southern California.

Printed in the USA
CPSIA information can be obtained
at www.ICGtesting.com
JSHW080749171123
51918JS00004B/33